ADRENALIN RUSH

WINDSURFING & KITE SURFING

ANNE-MARIE LAVAL

FRANKLIN WATTS
LONDON • SYDNEY

First published in 2012 by
Franklin Watts
338 Euston Road
London NW1 3BH

Franklin Watts Australia
Level 17/207 Kent Street
Sydney NSW 2000

Copyright © Franklin Watts 2012

All rights reserved.

Produced by Tall Tree Ltd

A CIP catalogue record for this book is available from the British Library.

Dewey Classification 796.9'39

ISBN: 978 1 4451 0479 9

Printed in China

Franklin Watts is a division of Hachette Children's Books, an Hachette UK company.

www.hachette.co.uk

Picture credits:
Cover, front: Dmitry Tsvetkov/Dreamstime.com
Cover, back: Rjmiguel/Dreamstime.com
1 Max Earey/Shutterstock, 4 Manolis Tsantakis/Dreamstime.com, 5 Pierre-yves Babelon/Dreamstime.com, 6 Patrick Ward/Corbis, 7t Hoch Zwei, 7b ohrim/Shutterstock, 8 Federico Donatini/Dreamstime.com, 9 Alexander Kolomietz/Dreamstime.com, 10 Dmitry Tsvetkov/Dreamstime.com, 11 sashagala/Shutterstock, 12-13 Tiziano Casalta/Dreamstime.com, 13t Tiziano Casalta/Dreamstime.com, 13b Juan Medina/Reuters/Corbis, 14 Paul Topp/Dreamstime.com, 15 Max Earey/ Shutterstock, 16 Ana del Castillo/Shutterstock, 17 ohrim/ Shutterstock, 18 Ben Welsh/Corbis, 19c Djo Vander Linden/Dreamstime.com, 19b Anna Chow/GNU, 20–21 Olga Makina/Dreamstime.com, 21 Adrien Freville, 22-23 Nomadz/GNU, 23t Gamma-Rapho/Getty Images, 23b Odyssée du Vent, 24-25 ADI WEDA/epa/Corbis, 25 Atm2003/Dreamstime.com, 26–27 Robert Hardholt/Shutterstock.com, 27 Ben Welsh/Corbis, 28 Pliene/Dreamstime.com, 29 Max Earey/Shutterstock.com

Disclaimer
The website addresses (URLs) included in this book were valid at the time of going to press. However, because of the nature of the Internet, it is possible that some addresses have changed, or sites may have changed or closed down since publication. While the author and publisher regret any inconvenience this may cause to readers, no responsibility for any such changes can be accepted either by the author or the publisher.

In preparation of this book, all due care has been exercised with regard to the advice, activities and techniques depicted. The publishers regret that they can accept no liability for any loss or injury sustained. When learning a new activity, it is important to get expert tuition and to follow a manufacturer's instructions.

Words in **bold** are in the glossary on page 30.

CONTENTS

Imagine skimming along the surface of the sea. The board under your feet skips across the **chop**, and suddenly you launch into the air for a massive jump. That is kite surfing or windsurfing: two different ways to get the same kind of thrill.

Windsurfing

Windsurfers use a surfboard-like board and a sail. The equipment is bulkier than kiting gear, but once the board and sail are rigged up, the thrill of skimming across the tops of the waves is mind-blowing. Windsurfing can also be done in very light winds – ones in which kites may not work.

A windsurfer uses a wave to flip himself into the air. Controlling the landing is the tricky bit, though!

Kite surfing

Kite surfers use large kites to drag their small boards across the sea, big lakes or even rivers. One of the advantages of kite surfing is that your equipment can be carried easily in a backpack, with your board under your arm. You can catch the bus to the beach, then go kiting!

A kite surfer skims along a lagoon in northern Madagascar.

Two top DVDs
- AC Extreme Kitesurfing – *some of the world's best kite surfers, including Mark Doyle and Aaron Hadlow, let rip in fantastic locations around the world.*
- KA1111 – *the first movie ever made by wavesailing genius Jason Polakow, this is now an all-time classic.*

ON THE SCREEN

A windsurfer stands by his board in the 1990s. By then boards had become much lighter and more fun to use.

Windsurfing and kite surfing are both quite new sports. Windsurfing took a while to become popular. Kite surfing took off very quickly after it appeared in the late 1990s.

Born in California, Robbie Naish moved to Hawaii when he was a small boy. He started windsurfing at 11, and won his first world title at 13 years old. He went on to win 10 more windsurfing world championships. In the 1990s, Naish got into the new sport of kite surfing, and won three further world titles.

The windsurfing craze

Windsurfing first became popular in the 1970s. Before then, if you wanted to go sailing you needed a boat. Windsurfers were far cheaper and easier to move around than boats. Even so, the original boards were heavy and hard to ride. The designs quickly improved, and in the 1980s windsurfing really took off. Suddenly, just about every beach in the world was decorated with brightly coloured sails.

Kite surfing kicks off

Kite surfing as we know it today developed in the 1990s, but kiting first became really popular in the 2000s. Today it is one of the fastest-growing ocean board sports. Many surfers are into kite surfing: when it's too windy to go surfing, the conditions are often ideal for kiting instead.

This kite surfer has managed to get on the water before his mates! He's riding a double-ended board, which is popular for tricks on flat water.

Windsurfing and kiting have split into lots of different disciplines. Which discipline people follow depends on whether they are sailing on the ocean or fresh water.

These windsurfers are racing on a lake in Italy. In the background you can see one of the course-marker buoys and a boat for the race officials.

Fresh water

Inland kiting and windsurfing mainly happen on lakes and reservoirs, as these have enough room for the riders to get going. Freshwater sailing tends to focus on **blasting** or **free riding**, as the waves are rarely big enough for more radical wave-sailing manoeuvres. However, a few rivers – such as the Hood River Gorge in the USA (see page 28) – offer advanced sailors the chance to show off their skills.

Kite surfers are attached to their kite by a harness. The harness spreads the force from the kite across the body, taking the strain away from the arms.

Don't try this at home
In the movie Die Another Day, secret agent James Bond kite surfs a car bonnet along a huge wave, using a parachute. This is a CGI stunt – it would be impossible in real life!

Ocean sailing

For both windsurfing and kite surfing, ocean sailing is divided into two key styles of riding: flat water and wave.

• On flat water, both kiters and windsurfers tend to focus on whizzing in and out from the beach at high speed, throwing in a spectacular jump or turn every once in a while. This is often called blasting or free riding.

• On waves, the emphasis is on either big jumps using the waves as launch ramps on the way out from the beach, or riding the waves like a super-powered surfer on the way back in.

The biggest difference between a windsurf board and a kite board is size. The smallest windsurf board is far bigger than the largest kite board. The sails and kites, of course, look completely different.

Windsurfing equipment

There are boards and sails for different conditions. The two extremes are wavesailing and light-wind windsurfing:

- Wavesailing uses a small board, and a sail with a high-cut foot (as shown here) so that it does not catch in the surf.

- Light-wind equipment includes a wide board and large sail with a low-cut foot.

Masts are usually made of carbon fibre and designed to bend as the sail is tensioned. Sails are made of lightweight, waterproof fabric.

Battens – strips of plastic inside sleeves that run across the sail – hold the sail in a nicely curved shape for catching the wind.

Boards are made of layers of tough material surrounding a foam core. Some boards have wooden decks to make them lighter.

Turned upside down, a kite can be carried easily by one person – if it was the right way up it could drag you into the air.

The kite gets its shape from tubes pumped full of air, like a bicycle tyre. They have to be tough and flexible enough to survive multiple crashes.

Kite surfing equipment

In kite surfing, the main choice of board is between one with footstraps, which is great for tricks and jumps, and one without. People select a kite depending on how windy it is. In lighter winds, a bigger kite is needed to get you moving. There are two main types of kite:

• Leading Edge Inflatables (LEIs), which have a straighter shape.

• Bow kites, which have a backward-curving shape. Bow kites can be used in a wider range of wind speeds than LEIs.

Top how-to DVDs
• Progression Kiteboarding – *this series of kite surfing DVDs is an excellent aid to learning, for everyone from complete beginners to experts.*
• Beginner to Winner – *renowned windsurfing coach Jen Hall takes the viewer from basic techniques to advanced skills.*

ON THE SCREEN

After a while, blasting in and out from the beach on your kite board just isn't enough. Even a long **downwinder** doesn't satisfy you. It's time to start throwing in some **freestyle** tricks – the techniques that make shore-bound spectators gasp in admiration.

Aerial action

Kite surfers get added **hang time** from the lifting action of the kite. Because the kite holds them up in the air, they seem to go into slow motion almost as soon as they take off. The most skilled riders use this hang time to perform amazing tricks.

Complicated freestyle spins and twists like these always draw 'Ooh' and 'Ahh' noises from people watching on the beach.

When something goes wrong, kite boarders let go of the bar they use to control the kite. This causes the kite to hover harmlessly in the air above them.

Freestyle tricks

These are some of the most popular types of freestyle trick:

• Grabs, in which the kite surfer holds the board with one hand.

• Spins, with the kite surfer spinning round and round in the air.

• Board-offs, in which the rider takes one or both feet off the board.

• Inverts, the name for any trick done upside down.

• Kite loops, in which the rider loops the kite through 360 degrees while doing a spin.

Aaron Hadlow is probably the best freestyle kite surfer ever. He first won the PKRA world championship at just 15 years old, and went on to win four more titles in a row. Since 2010 he has taken a break from contests, but is sure to be back on the water soon.

AARON HADLOW

One of the most exciting forms of windsurfing is wavesailing. At surf spots around the world, from Hawaii to the Canary Islands to Australia, you see excited windsurfers **rigging up** on days when the wind is blowing and the surf is up

In wavesailing, a vertical takeoff like this can only mean one thing: this windsurfer is trying to do a loop.

Wavesailing part 1: getting out

For surfers, getting out to where the waves are breaking usually involves a long, hard paddle. For windsurfers, however, getting out is half the fun. The sailors time their run so that a **whitewater** wave doesn't smash them back into shore. Once clear of the whitewater, the waves sloping into shore provide ramps for launching all kinds of aerials. The most spectacular are loops and barrel rolls, in which the board, sail and sailor all go end-over-end through 360 degrees.

With the power of a sail, windsurfers are able to do things on waves that ordinary surfers can only dream of. They speed around sections of whitewater, make powerful turns, and slide along the tops of waves.

Wavesailing part 2: coming in

Riding a wave back in, the windsurfers pull off similar moves to surfers. They have the advantage of a sail to power them along, but the sail can get caught in the wave and cause a **wipeout**. Key wave-riding moves include:

• Bottom turns, when the sailor banks the board over at the base of the wave.

• Off-the-lips, when the sailor does a turn off the top of the wave and drops down the **face**.

• Cutbacks, where the sailor does a tight turn to come back in the opposite direction.

Kite boarders have been taking to the surf pretty much since the sport was invented. Even in small, choppy waves kite boarding is great fun – but when the surf picks up and starts to roll into the beach in clean lines, things really start to hot up.

Why surf kiting rocks

Surf kiting has advantages over both surfing and windsurfing. It's easier and more fun to get out past the breaking waves than the long paddle of surfing. And on the way back in, if you get into any trouble on a kite board, there's a good chance you will be able to use the kite's lift to get yourself out of trouble again.

Surf kiting techniques

The techniques kite surfers use combine surfing, windsurfing and skateboarding tricks, together with some things you can only do on a kite board.

One move only kite surfers can do is called an aerial floater, which gets them over a section of whitewater. Using the power of the kite, they can cover much bigger distances than would be possible on a surfboard alone.

Even on a kite board, getting out through the breaking waves can be a challenge.

Two top surf movies
- *Big Windy – filmed over an extended period in the Pacific islands, this movie combines an environmental message with some of the best wave riding ever seen.*
- *Cape Reels – shot in and around Cape Town, South Africa, this movie's highlight is probably the **offshore** big-wave action; there is plenty of smaller surf and freestyle fun too.*

ON THE SCREEN

Surfers have ridden big waves for many years. But the biggest waves – over 15 metres tall – are impossible for a surfer to catch in the usual way. So surfers began to develop the idea of tow-in surfing. Being towed up to speed would let them catch bigger waves than ever before.

*This rider is doing a beautiful off-the-lip **carve**. Timing is everything on a kite board. The kite must be pulling hard at just the right moment for a spectacular move like this one.*

Tow-in surfing develops

In Hawaii in the 1990s, big-wave surfers such as Laird Hamilton and Manu Bertin began to spread the popularity of kite surfing. Some big-wave surfers had the idea of using powerful kites to build up the speed needed to catch giant waves. However, they quickly moved on to using **wave runners**. These had the advantage that the towline from the wave runner could be dropped once the wave had been caught.

Big-wave kiting today

Even though dedicated big-wave surfers no longer use kites, kite surfers still regularly tow themselves into the world's biggest surf. Kites are often spotted in the lineups at famous big-wave spots such as Mavericks in California, Todos Santos (Mexico), Dungeons (South Africa) and Log Cabins (Hawaii).

Kite surfers can use waves like large, moving ramps. This kite surfer is performing a move called a lip bash, sending up a plume of water behind his board.

Laird Hamilton was brought up in Hawaii, where he quickly became an excellent surfer. Hamilton is today known as one of the all-time great big-wave surfers, as well as one of the inventors of tow-in surfing. His most famous wave was one he rode at Teahupoo in Tahiti, in 2000. The wave was so big, thick and fast that it is often called, 'the heaviest wave ever ridden'.

LAIRD HAMILTON

One of the fiercest rivalries between kite surfers and windsurfers is to see who can go fastest. For many years, windsurfers held the outright speed record for wind-powered watercraft. But when kite boarding hit the scene, things soon changed.

Windsurfers blasting back to the beach at Dahab, Egypt, where every year you can see some of the fastest sailors in the world.

Kite surfing rules

In 2010, kite surfers grabbed the high-speed crown with a speed of 54.10 **knots**. This is 100.19 kph – it was the first time any wind-powered craft had broken the 100 kph barrier. That same year kite surfers broke the record twice more, ending with a record speed of 55.65 knots (103.06 kph). In the meantime, windsurfing had fallen behind: the last time it held the speed record was in 2008, with a speed of 49.09 knots.

Lüderitz, Namibia

The ding-dong battle for the speed record has been fought out largely at Lüderitz in Namibia. There, calm water and fiercely strong winds combine to create the best speed-sailing conditions on Earth. The racers don't have to worry about the great white sharks that haunt the ocean off Lüderitz – they're going too fast for a great white to catch them!

American kite surfer Rob Douglas sets a new world speed record at the 2010 Lüderitz Speed Challenge.

Speed records 2008–10

Year:	Type of craft:	Place:	Speed (in knots):
2008	Windsurfer	Stes Maries de la Mer, France	49.09
2008	Kite surfer	Lüderitz , Namibia	49.84
2008	Kite surfer	Lüderitz , Namibia	50.26
2008	Kite surfer	Lüderitz , Namibia	50.57
2009	Hydrofoil trimaran	Hyeres, France	51.36
2010	Kite surfer	Lüderitz , Namibia	54.10
2010	Kite surfer	Lüderitz , Namibia	55.49
2010	Kite surfer	Lüderitz , Namibia	55.65

Most people enjoy going windsurfing or kite surfing for an hour or two. Then they go home and have something to eat and a shower. For some, however, this just isn't enough. They decide to race across large stretches of water or even spend weeks crossing huge oceans.

Long-distance ladies

Female kiters have made some of the most amazing long-distance kite crossings:

- Three-times world wave kiting champion Kirsty Jones set a new record in 2006, when she crossed the 225 km from the Canary Islands to Morocco in just 9 hours.

- In 2010, Natalie Clarke kited 240 km across Australia's Bass Strait in 9.5 hours.

- Also in 2010, Louise Tapper set a world record by kiting 2,000 km in 23 days.

Even kite surfing across a narrow channel like this one for an hour or two is hard work. Imagine being a record-breaking long-distance kiter and travelling hundreds of kilometres for hours on end!

Frenchman Arnauld de Rosnay was one of the first sailors to push the limits of how far a windsurfer could go. His adventures included:
• Sailing down the coast of the Sahara region.
• Crossing the Bering Strait.
• Making the voyage from Florida to Cuba.
De Rosnay disappeared in 1984, while trying to cross the Straits of Formosa between China and Taiwan.

Windsurfing across oceans

Windsurfers, with hulls modified to allow the sailor to sleep in them, have made some huge long-distance trips:

• In 1997, American Steve Fisher sailed from California to Hawaii by windsurfer.

• In 2003, Frenchwoman Raphaela le Gouvello made a crossing from Peru to Tahiti. In 2006, she crossed the Indian Ocean.

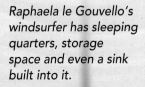

Raphaela le Gouvello's windsurfer has sleeping quarters, storage space and even a sink built into it.

There are all kinds of windsurfing and kite surfing competitions. They range from the contest you have with your friends to see who can get to a buoy fastest to big world championships for **pros**.

Windsurfing competition

Competitive windsurfers either have to be good at going fast or controlling the board.

- If they are good at going fast, either one-design racing (in which everyone uses the same design of board and sail) or slalom (racing around a course marked out with buoys) might appeal. One-design racing can take you all the way to the Olympics, where it is one of the hotly contested sailing events.

- If windsurfers are good at board control, there is a choice between wave riding and freestyle contests.

The giant sails used in one-design racing make the sailors look tiny.

Kite surfing contests

The most popular kite surfing contests are for wave riding and freestyle. These are the competitions that draw the biggest crowds, because they feature spectacular aerials, carves and, of course, high-speed crashes. There are also races around a pre-set course, hang time contests to see who can stay in the air longest, and competitions featuring kickers and sliders (ramps placed in the water).

Competitors wait on the beach for a kite surfing contest to begin.

The fresh air and exercise of windsurfing and kiting are good for you. They get you fitter and healthier than sitting at home playing computer games. But kiting and windsurfing can also be dangerous, so guidelines have been developed to help keep everyone safe.

Get instruction

It's always a good idea to get specialist instruction when learning a new sport. This is especially true with activities like windsurfing and kiting, which happen in a dangerous environment and with unfamiliar equipment. A qualified instructor makes sure that everyone learns in the safest way possible, without putting themselves or others in danger.

This kite surfer has realised it's all gone wrong and 'bailed' – let go of the kite's control bar and started to kick off his board.

Ride within your abilities

Windsurfing and kiting attract daredevil personalities. They may be tempted to push themselves, and go out in conditions that are harder than they are used to. This is never a good idea. People may be able to cope at first, but the wind or waves could pick up, drop or change direction. Getting into difficulties and having to be rescued puts other people in danger, as well as yourself.

Respect other people

Share the water with everyone else: other kite surfers, windsurfers, sailors, canoeists, surfers, swimmers, paddlers – everyone. They all have a right to be there, so never get grumpy because it's too crowded. If you don't like the crowds, leave – but don't expect other people to get out of your way.

Even the best windsurfers get it wrong sometimes. The important thing is to make sure no one else gets hurt by your mistakes!

Rules of the road
- *When another sailor or kiter is coming towards you, always pass them to your right.*
- *Never kite surf or windsurf in a wind blowing straight offshore.*
- *When two kiters are sailing along (in the same or opposite directions), the upwind kite surfer should keep his or her **lines** high, to avoid getting tangled in the downwind kite's lines.*

Imagine you won the lottery, and could book a round-the-world ticket to go on a dream trip. Where would you stop off for some windsurfing or kite surfing kicks? There are hundreds of great places, but this list should give you a few ideas about where to start.

Tarifa, Spain

Probably the windsurfing and kite surfing capital of Europe, Tarifa sits on the far south coast of Spain, looking across the sea to Africa. Almost every afternoon the wind picks up, and spectators are treated to the sight of some of the world's best sailors and kiters practising their moves.

Hood River Gorge, USA

The Gorge is an unusual place for high-performance windsurfing and kite surfing, because it is a river rather than an ocean or lake. There are wide stretches of water, spots with waves, places that are better for beginners, and high average wind speeds.

Kite surfing in the cool, clear waters of Tarifa in Spain, which many people think is the best place for wind and kite surfing in Europe.

Ho'okipa, Hawaii

One guidebook says that 'Ho'okipa is to windsurfers what Mount Everest is to mountaineers'. This place on the island of Maui is one every wave sailor dreams of going. It's not for the faint-hearted, though – wipe out and there is a good chance you will be washed onto the rocks.

Diamond Head, Hawaii

Diamond Head is known as the best place for wavesailing on the island of Oahu. Any time the wind blows there will be people rigging up brightly coloured wave sails and carrying their boards down to the beach to test themselves in the surf.

Margaret River, Australia

One of Australia's most famous big-wave spots, Margaret River is not a place for beginner windsurfers or kite surfers. The surf here can be huge, and the reefs make it a dangerous place to be washed ashore by big waves. It's a great place to watch the action, though, even if you don't go out.

Lake Arenal, Costa Rica

Created by a hydroelectric dam built in 1973, this giant lake took three years to fill up. Today, it is a high-wind destination for windsurfers and kiters between November and April, and is excellent for freestyle and blasting.

Want to ride the biggest surf, surrounded by the world's best riders? Then head for the Hawaiian island of Maui.

blasting

windsurfing or kite surfing in a more-or-less straight line, going as fast as possible while throwing in turns, jumps or other moves.

carve

turn made with the board leaning right over, throwing up a sheet of spray.

chop

little bumps on the surface of the water created by the wind blowing across it.

downwinder

kite surfing from one place to another that is further downwind, which allows you to travel quickly and easily.

face

front part of a wave, before it has broken (crumbled down on itself).

free riding

see blasting.

freestyle

form of windsurfing or kite surfing that features jumps, slides, spins and other tricks.

hang time

time spent in the air while doing a jump.

knots

units for measuring speed at sea or in the air; one knot is 1.85 kph.

lines

strong cords connecting a kite surfer to his or her kite.

offshore

away from the shore; out to sea.

pros

professionals, people who are paid to do something as their job.

rigging up

putting a windsurfer together ready to go out sailing.

wave runners

powered water craft designed to carry one or two people, a bit like ocean-going motorbikes.

whitewater

the foamy water that appears when a wave breaks.

wipeout

crash while surfing, windsurfing or kite surfing.

Competitions and organizations

The kite surfing world championships are run by the Pro Kiteboard Riders Association (PKRA). There are competitions for wave riding, freestyle and course racing. The contests are held all round the world, at some of the best spots on Earth for kiting. You can find out more at http://www.prokitetour.com.

The Professional Windsurfers Association (PWA) organizes some of the world's top-level professional windsurfing contests. As in kite surfing, there are contests for wave riding, freestyle and course racing. Events take place all around the world, but most are held in Europe, where windsurfing is especially popular. Find out more at http://www.pwaworldtour.com.

Language and terminology

Working out what an expert is talking about when he or she describes a kite surfing trick or a piece of windsurfing equipment can be difficult. These two websites help:

www.prokitetour.com/terminology-and-tricks-definition.php

www.windsurfing-academy.com/start_windsurfing/ why_windsurfing/beginner/windsurfing_glossary.asp

Long-distance windsurfing

Look at the website of one of the best long-distance windsurfers ever, Raphaela le Gouvello. It contains an excellent technical guide to what you have to do to survive a windsurfing journey hundreds of kilometres long:

www.raphaela-legouvello.com

INDEX

These are the lists of contents for each title in Adrenalin Rush:

Snowboarding
Hitting the slopes • The birth of snowboarding • Snowboarding today • Snowboard design • Equipment and clothing • Piste riding • Big air • Boardercross • Riding freestyle • Freeriding fun • Staying alive • Snowboard hotspots • Extreme snowboarding

MTB
Hit the dirt • Pioneers of MTB • MTB conquers the world • Types of bike • Equipment and clothing • Cross-country • Cross-country racing • Long-haul heroes • North Shore style • Four-cross • Downhill racers • Staying alive • Mountain bike hotspots

BMX
One gear is plenty • BMX takes over the world • The rebirth of BMX • Bike love • Equipment and clothing • Street riding • Ramps and vert riding • Flatland skills • Dirt jumping • BMX racing • Racetrack skills • Staying alive • BMX hotspots

Skateboarding
Hitting the concrete • Pioneers of skating • Conquering the world • Board meeting • Equipment and clothing • Street skating • Ramping up • Vert and mega ramps • Flatland tricks • Longboard riding • Going downhill – fast! • Staying alive • Skateboard hotspots